The QUILTER'S WORKBOOK

Pam Lintott &
Rosemary Miller

First published in 1993
by Charles Letts & Co Ltd
Letts of London House
Parkgate Road
London SW11 4NQ

Created and produced by Rosemary Wilkinson
4 Lonsdale Square, London N1 1EN

Art editor: Frances de Rees
Illustrators: Terry Evans, Richard Hawke, Mark Scribbens
Photographers: Mark Gatehouse, Shona Wood

A CIP catalogue record for this book is available from the British Library.

'Letts' is a registered trademark of Charles Letts & Co Limited

ISBN 1 85238 422 0

Typeset by Get Set Typesetting, Dorking, Surrey

Printed in Singapore

CONTENTS

THE FOLLOWING PAGES ARE BLANK
FOR YOUR OWN NOTES:
17, 29, 66-69, 78-81, 96-97, 100-101

ABOUT THE AUTHORS

Pam Lintott and Rosemary Miller have owned The Quilt Room in Dorking, Surrey, since 1981. When they opened the shop they little dreamed how successful it would become but since then the craft of patchwork and quilting has undergone an amazing revival becoming ever more popular.

From the beginning, people have come to the shop for advice on quiltmaking, so the workshops which are now held three times a week above the shop in the winter were a natural development. They bring tutors from all over the country each to teach their own specialised techniques.

Pam's interest in quilts began back in the 1970s when she was living in America. Subsequent travels around the world seeing other forms of patchwork and quilting fuelled her interest. For Pam the wonderful thing about patchwork is that there is a technique for everyone and as her lifestyle has changed so have the techniques she favours. When she was living on a boat with lots of time on her hands (but not a lot of space) she used to handstitch hexagons; when her children were small and time was more precious she began machine sewing and now, when there is hardly any time at all, she uses rotary cutting techniques which are the fastest of all. How many hobbies can be so adaptable?

Although Rosemary first learnt the basics of needlework from her mother, she went on, after school, to train in catering, and was a successful freelance cook before and during the early part of her marriage until the arrival of her children. Several years later, she saw a beautiful quilt at a friend's house, and this inspired her to start making her own, which was the beginning of an enthralling hobby - and a thriving business! Rosemary's love of fabrics, and the matching and blending of their colours, together with the element of mathematical calculations, make quilting for her a most challenging and creative hobby.

HOW TO USE THIS WORKBOOK

This workbook intersperses facts and figures on quiltmaking, based on the questions we are most frequently asked in the shop, with pages on which you can record your own notes and discoveries. We build from our own experience; we learn from experimenting, and if these findings aren't written down, it is so easy to forget - especially if that quilt which turned out so well ends up on the other side of the world.

We have included worksheets listing all the important details of your quilts and suggest a photo is also taken and kept with the workbook. Use the worksheets from the minute you start planning your quilt until you have proudly signed it. Remember to note any problems that may occur as this will assist in future quilts. If you use up all the worksheets in the workbook please feel free to photocopy more.

As well as explaining exactly how to work out fabric quantities, we have included charts for many of the more popular patchwork shapes and these will tell you at a glance how much fabric you will require.

We have made a number of different blocks in different colourways just to give ideas. Templates for these blocks are not included - after reading about drafting templates they should all be within your reach. You will recognise some of the blocks - others are not so well known. We have sewn four blocks together so you can see the interesting secondary designs many of the blocks form once joined. This is not always obvious when looking at just a single block.

There's information on colour and fabric preparation, as well as brief details on hand and machine patchwork, quilting patterns and appliqué techniques. The section on antique quilts gives clues on dating and finally there's a collection of tips containing lots of snippets of information which we hope you will find interesting.

Metric equivalents throughout the book have been rounded up or down to give workable measurements rather than exact conversions, so always work with one set of measurements only.

Enjoy the workbook and enjoy your quilting.

QUILT HISTORY

Quiltmaking is an ancient craft and although its beginnings cannot be traced precisely, there is a Sicilian quilt dating from around 1400 in the Victoria & Albert Museum. During the Middle Ages soldiers wore a quilted garment under their chain mail for added protection both against the harsh winters and from flying arrows. It is also documented that in May 1540 Katherine Howard, one of Henry VIII's wives, received twenty-three quilts out of the Royal Wardrobe as a sign of royal favour before her marriage.

The main historical types of quilting in England were appliqué, which was often combined with elaborate embroidery, and mosaic patchwork, which was sewn over papers. This technique of sewing over papers is still popular today and referred to as "English patchwork". Of all the design pieces used in patchwork the hexagon has proved to be the one with the most staying power: from the hexagon quilts of the early 1700s right through to the present day. Certain areas of Britain, most notably Durham, Wales and Northumberland, also became famous for beautifully fine quilting on wholecloth or strip quilts.

When the Pilgrim Fathers arrived in America in 1621 they certainly had more than a few quilts stored in their holds, though not in the repeated block format that we think of today as American patchwork. Britain had wanted to protect its own textile industry and had not allowed looms or other tools of the textile industry to be exported, so fabrics could not be manufactured elsewhere and all textiles had to be shipped from the mother country. Thus new fabric was a luxury few in the New World could afford. The repeated block method probably evolved as it was time-saving and easier to sew in the

This late nineteenth century American quilt has the Texas Star block as the central medallion, surrounded by a variety of borders.

limited spaces in which many of the settlers lived. Individual blocks could be worked in the lap, then sewn together when all were completed.

When the settlers of the New World ventured into the West, quilting became a part of the lifestyle of the pioneer women. They developed new designs for quilt blocks and gave them names which reflected the fortunes and hardships of their daily life as well as private political affiliations (women were not allowed to vote): names such as *Bear's Paw*, *Indian Hatchet*, *Barn Raising*, *Corn & Beans*, *Broken Dishes*, *Whig Rose*, *Lincoln's Platform* and probably the best-known of all - *Log Cabin*.

It wasn't until the mid 1970s that the American form of patchwork began to become popular in Britain.

CLUES TO DATING QUILTS

D ating quilts is not a very precise science especially if we try to do it by dating the fabric. We all know how long a favourite piece can sit in our fabric cupboard before being used. There are of course certain fabrics which are instantly recognisable but even these cannot give us any precise dates, they merely fix the earliest time that a quilt could have been made. Turkey Red, which is so distinctly recognisable in antique quilts, dates back to 1780. The novelty of being able to use this deep red without the risk of the dye running appealed to quilters and the combination of Turkey Red and white became extremely popular for both pieced and appliquéd quilts in the mid-nineteenth century. Chintz fabric with exotic flower and tree designs brought over from India was highly prized and much in demand all through the seventeenth and eighteenth centuries. The motifs were cut out and appliquéd onto a background fabric: this technique being known as Broderie Perse. In response to this, in the early nineteenth century, the textile industry began producing printed squares of fabric especially for medallion quilts and borders.

The style of patchwork can be a useful clue since designs went in and out of popularity in the same way as other fashions. Again, though, there is no guarantee of accuracy as patterns from one era were obviously picked up and used at later dates. Medallion quilts were one of the earliest styles of quilts and they often featured appliquéd flowers and birds. Crazy quilts became popular in 1880 and were fashionable all through Victorian times becoming increasingly more ornate as time went on.

The sewing machine was invented around 1850 and did not really become well used until around 1870. Obviously all machine stitched quilts would be later than this date. Before the early 1900s the edges of quilts were mainly straight but with the advent of commercially-produced bias binding curved and scalloped edges became very popular.

What has to be done therefore is to consider the fabric, design and the make-up of the quilt and even then we will only arrive at an approximate date.

TYPES OF QUILTS

Amish Quilts An American style of patchwork made by the Amish community in Pennsylvania, Indiana and Ohio, characterised by bright, bold, plain fabrics pieced together in simple geometric designs, usually with a large quantity of black. The quilts are heavily quilted in intricate patterns with fine stitches.

Baltimore Album Quilts During the mid-nineteenth century ladies of Baltimore, Maryland, U.S.A., made quilts memorialising events and people. A typical quilt comprised many different appliqué techniques and in one block there might be as many as a hundred separate pieces. They were mainly in reds, greens and yellows on a cream background, each block being made and signed by a different person. These old appliqué techniques have been revived and beautiful quilts are again being produced.

Charm Quilts are quilts where no two pieces are made from the same fabric and only one simple template is used. Fabric collections for these quilts are often swapped among friends.

Crazy Quilts A random arrangement of many irregular-shaped fabric pieces which became very popular in Victorian times. The pieces are often in a variety of colours and textures, the edges of the patches being secured and disguised with embroidery, usually feather stitch.

Friendship/Album Quilts These are presentation quilts. Each block is made by a different person with a space for inscribing a motto or saying and a signature. The blocks are then assembled and the finished quilt is presented to a member of a group as a memento.

Medallion Quilts These form one of the earliest types of patchwork. Each quilt has a large central motif surrounded by several different blocks and borders radiating outwards.

Sampler Quilts All the blocks in a sampler quilt are different which makes it an interesting quilt for beginners, as they will learn a wide variety of techniques in their first quilt.

Scrap Quilts These quilts are made, as the name suggests, entirely of scraps, often set with a calico background. Originally the scraps were pieces left over from dressmaking so the quilts could contain fabric from childhood to adulthood thereby making a quilt full of mèmories.

Wholecloth Quilts These consist of two large pieces of fabric with wadding between. Often the back and front are in contrasting colours. They are elaborately quilted with traditional designs.

A charming American "Double Wedding Ring" scrap quilt from the 1920s. It was probably made for someone's wedding.

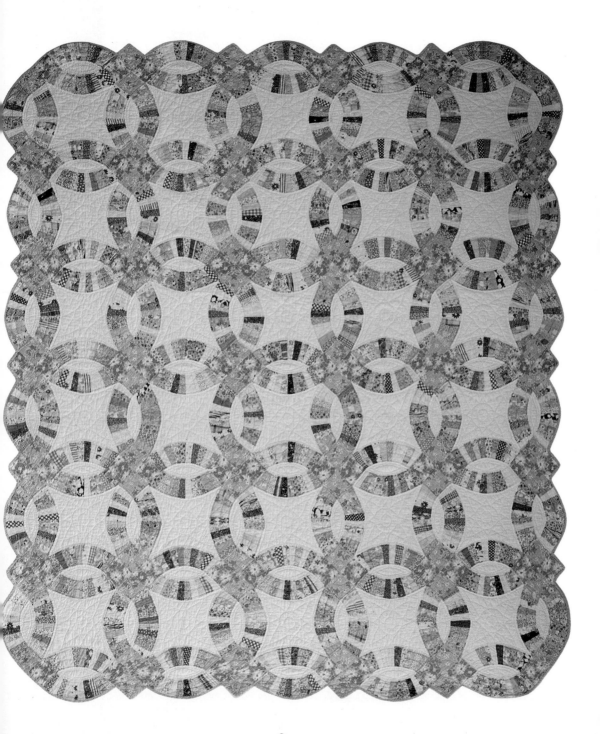

CARE OF QUILTS

All fabric deteriorates with age and is affected by light, so keep quilts away from strong daylight.

Dust and dirt can rot the fibres of a quilt. One way of removing surface dust is to gently vacuum the quilt. This is a good solution for quilts that can neither be washed nor dry cleaned.

If it is known that the fabrics in a quilt have been pre-washed, then it is safe to wash it gently in the washing machine using a mild detergent. The water should be no hotter than 30°C/86°F and only a short spin should be used.

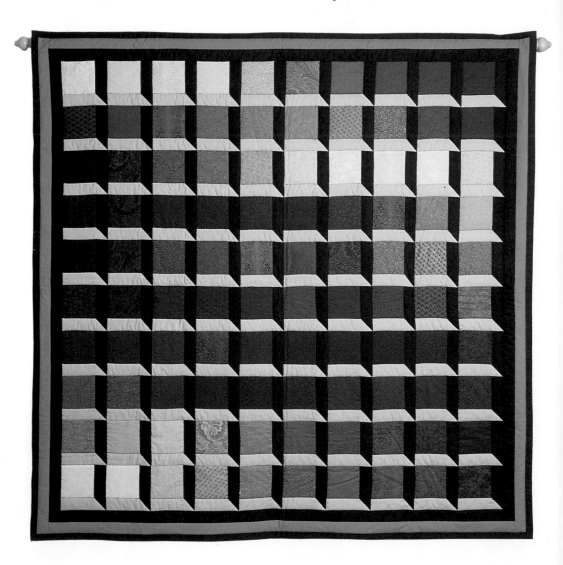

Avoid biological washing powders at all costs. You can dry a quilt in a large tumble dryer on low heat. Place a dry bath towel in with it to assist drying and prevent it from twisting. Remove while still damp, and lay out flat to dry to prevent creasing.

If the quilt is very large it can be hand washed in the bath. After the final rinse gently press out as much water as possible but do not squeeze or wring out. The quilt will be very heavy at this stage and care must be taken not to break any sewing or quilting stitches. Carefully lift the quilt onto bath towels and press out any excess moisture.

The quilt must be dried flat, laid right side down on a large sheet. This can be done outside on a clear day.

Dry-cleaning is a tough process but if the fabrics have not been pre-washed and there is a chance of the colours running it can be done. Ask the cleaners not to press the quilt. Hang it out to air until the fumes have gone.

STORAGE

If you have room always roll a quilt round a cardboard tube covered with acid-free paper. Otherwise fold the quilt over acid-free paper and store in a pillow case which allows the fabric to breathe. It should be re-folded every few months ensuring that the fold lines are made in different places. Never store quilts in plastic bags.

DISPLAYING QUILTS

When displaying quilts it is important that the weight of the quilt is evenly distributed. Use this method for making a sleeve to hold a pole or batten and the quilt will hang well without pulling on any particular point.

1   Cut a 6 in (15 cm) strip of fabric the width of your quilt. This might have to be pieced. Hem the raw edges on the short sides. Stitch the long sides together and turn right side out to form a tube or sleeve.

2   Position the sleeve at the back of the quilt with the top edge of the sleeve just below the bottom edge of the quilt

Left: The block design of this wallhanging is "Attic Windows". It has been made using one hundred fabrics from the Jinny Beyer Palette.

binding. Sew by hand to the back of the quilt along the top and bottom of the sleeve, being careful that the stitches do not go through to the front of the quilt. Insert pole or batten and hang from supports at each end.

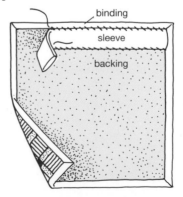

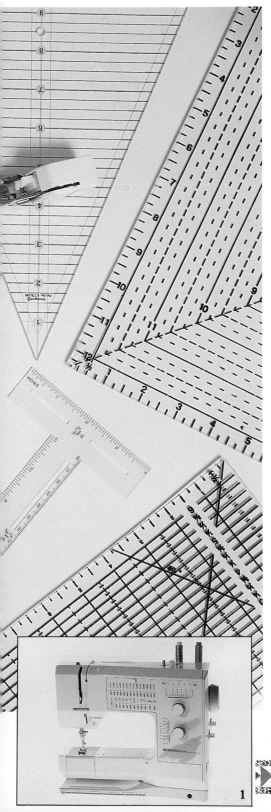

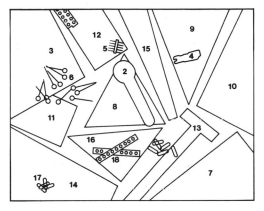

Rotary Cutting and Machine Piecing Equipment

1. Sewing machine
2. Rotary cutter
3. Cutting mat
4. Walking foot
5. Sewing machine needles
6. Flat-headed pins
7. Quilter's ruler
8. 60 degree triangle
9. Right-angled triangle
10. 12½ in square lap board (for squaring up blocks)
11. Bi-Rangle (for forming half-rectangles)
12. Scrap-saver (for cutting squares, rectangles and triangles)
13. T-square
14. Pineapple ruler (for accuracy in cutting pineapple blocks)
15. 9 degree circle wedge ruler (for bargello)
16. 45 degree kaleidoscope ruler (for forming kaleidoscope blocks)
17. Safety pins
18. Fabric grips

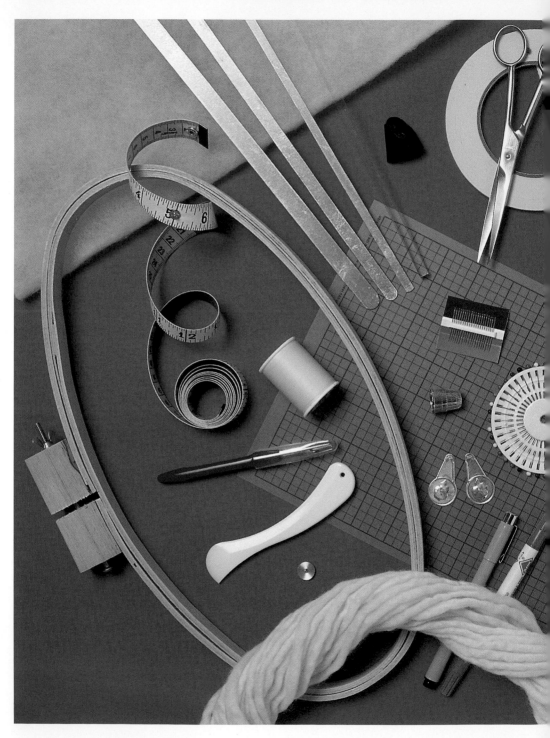

14

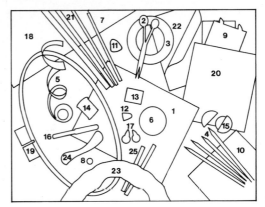

Patchwork and Quilting Equipment

1. Gridded template plastic
2. Scissors
3. Masking tape
4. Marking pencils
5. Tape measure
6. Glass headed pins
7. Quilter's quarter (for marking ¼ in seam allowance)
8. Dream seamer (for marking ¼ in seam allowance on curves)
9. Mirror imaging (to see your block repeated)
10. Multi-view lens (to see your block repeated 25 times)
11. Leather thimble
12. Raised-edge thimble
13. Betweens needles (for quilting)
14. Quilting thread
15. Beeswax
16. Seam ripper
17. Needle threader
18. Wadding
19. Quilting hoop
20. Quilting stencil
21. Bias bars (for bias appliqué)
22. Freezer paper
23. Quilting wool (for trapunto work)
24. Hera marker (another way of marking your quilting design)
25. Pigma pen (for signing quilts)

ELEMENTS OF A QUILT

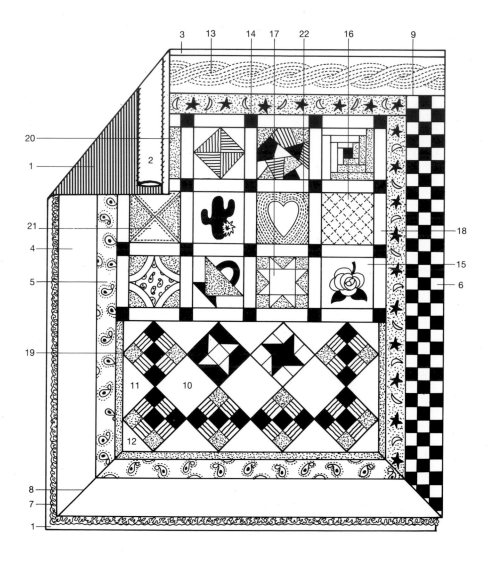

1	Backing	7	Wadding	13	Quilted border	19	On point setting
2	Sleeve	8	Mitred corner	14	Sashing square	20	Straight setting
3	Binding	9	Straight corner	15	Appliqué block	21	Outline quilting
4	Outer border	10	Alternate block	16	Grid quilting	22	Echo quilting
5	Inner border	11	Setting triangle	17	Pieced block		
6	Pieced border	12	Corner triangle	18	Sashing strip		

NOTES

COLOUR

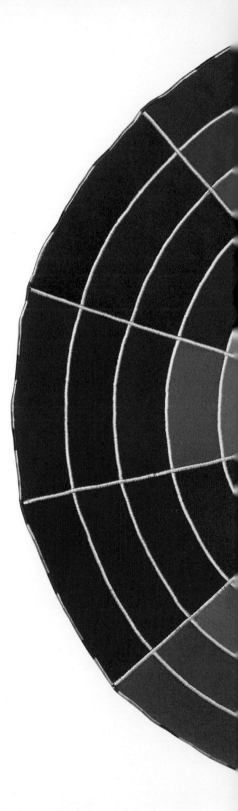

A little knowledge of colour and its effects can be very useful but do not let too much theory subdue your own natural flair and ability. The twelve basic colours are usually displayed in a circle or wheel. They are made up of three groups of colours.

Primary colours - red, yellow and blue. These cannot be obtained by mixing - they are pure colours. They form the points of an equilateral triangle on the Colour Wheel.

Secondary colours - orange, green and purple. These are made by mixing equal proportions of two adjacent primary colours.

red + yellow = orange
yellow + blue = green
red + blue = purple

Tertiary colours. These are formed by combining equal proportions of one primary colour and one of its secondary colours.

yellow + orange = yellow-orange
red + orange = red-orange
red + purple = red-purple
blue + purple = blue-purple
blue + green = blue-green
yellow + green = yellow-green

Tints. The pure colours on the Colour Wheel can be lightened by adding white - they are then called tints.

Shades. By adding black the colours are darkened and are called shades.

Tones. Grey added to colours produces a dulled hue - it becomes less intense.

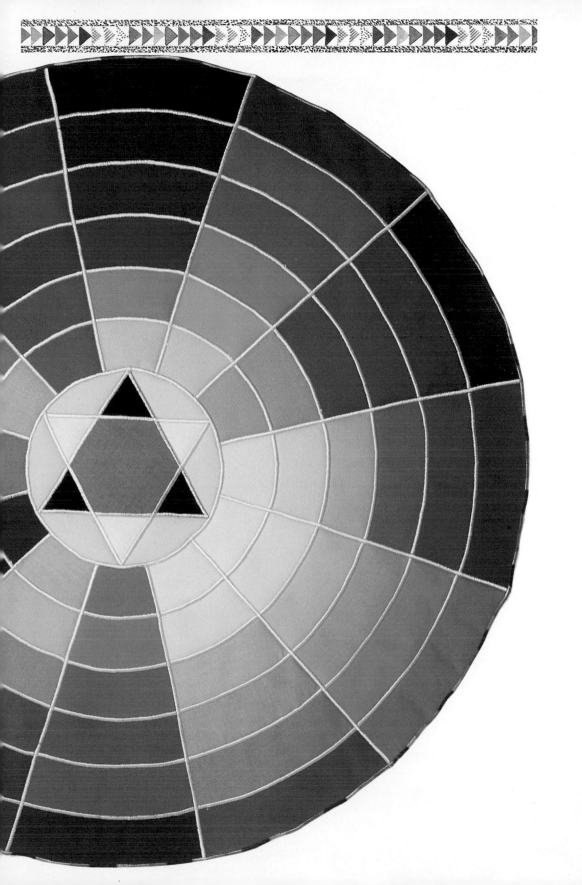

COLOUR - VALUE - SCALE

Colour

Most people have a vague idea what basic colour they want their quilt to be. This normally depends on the existing decoration of the room in which it is going to be displayed, whether on wall or bed. However, you need several different fabrics to produce a well-balanced quilt and this is often where the problems arise. There are a number of colour combinations to consider:

Monochromatic A monochromatic scheme consists of only one colour but can include different values of that colour, e.g. if you want a red quilt you could extend from pale pinks to burgundy. This is a safe choice especially for a beginner, possibly adding a small amount of a complementary colour (see below) to add interest.

Analogous This uses colours adjacent to each other on a section of the Colour Wheel. The section should not be too large, certainly not more than half the circle, e.g. with your red fabric you could extend from blues through to red or possibly purple through to orange. These adjacent colours harmonise well. Different values (see below) can be added and also neutrals.

Complementary (or contrasting) A scheme using colours opposite to each other on the Colour Wheel. Complementary colours used in equal proportions can be very dramatic, for example a red and green quilt would be stunning. Complementary colours used in unequal proportions can also be a very good combination as the colour used in the smaller proportion becomes the accent and will add a touch of sparkle. For example a touch of rust (orange) added to a blue quilt can bring it to life.

An Achromatic quilt would consist only of black, white and grey.

Value

Value is the degree of lightness or darkness in a colour. Value is the most important consideration when choosing fabrics - even more so than colour. Without the contrast between light, medium and dark your quilt will not look good. Value is relative, so it is not until you put your fabrics together that the right balance can be judged. Using a reducing glass or looking through the wrong end of binoculars can help in checking relative values but standing back from your fabrics and squinting is very effective.

Scale

This refers to the size of the pattern or motif on a printed fabric. The small print has long been very popular with quiltmakers although the designers of antique quilts seem to have been far more adventurous, sometimes using quite outrageous fabrics to great effect. We are now beginning to explore the possibilities of large scale prints again, producing exciting combinations and adding new dimensions to our quilts.

FABRIC SELECTION

To be confronted by bolts and bolts of fabric often confuses even the most experienced quiltmaker. Don't panic. Look around and pick out one fabric that you really like. Try to find one that includes a number of the colours you want in your quilt, or that contains the basic colour you had in mind. For a beginner, it is simplest to start with a mixture of just three or four fabrics. When choosing the fabrics to accompany your first choice, always remember the three important points: **colour – value – scale**

Featuring the "Pineapple" block, this modern quilt was made with the aid of a rotary cutter and the sewing machine. It is machine pieced and quilted.

The fabric choices should combine to produce a balance which is harmonious but not too predictable.

A mixture of printed and plain fabrics will produce an interesting quilt. Try mixing plains, large and small prints, geometric designs, plaids and striped fabrics. Patches cut out of border prints can be rejoined to give stunning effects. You can always use the wrong side of a fabric to get just that perfect colour for your project. From a distance a small print can appear to be a plain colour, it is only on close inspection that the print can be seen adding extra interest. Check your fabric selection from close up and at a distance.

Plains tend to be stronger in value than prints. Try dyeing your own to get beautiful graduated shades. You don't always have to use a neutral colour as a background. Black or a dark background can be dramatic especially for a modern colour scheme.

Some colours have a warm effect on the viewers, others a cool one:
– red, orange, yellow are warm colours;
– green, blue and purple are cool colours.
When combined warm colours come to the foreground and appear larger, while cool colours recede.

The addition of a cool accent to a warm quilt or a warm accent to a cool quilt can be just what is needed to balance a quilt.

FABRIC PREPARATION

All cotton fabric is made up of two woven threads. The lengthwise thread is called the warp and is taut with little or no give. The widthwise thread that runs from selvage to selvage is called the weft and has a little give. Selvages are the edges of the fabric and these must be removed before using. A cut made diagonally across the warp and the weft is made "on the bias". Fabric stretches on the bias, therefore when cutting fabric for patchwork care should be taken to place templates on the straight of the grain, i.e. parallel to the warp or the weft threads.

Washing
Wash fabric before it is used in patchwork. This will remove all sizing and loose dye and will shrink the fabric before it is sewn. Unfold all fabric. Separate the darks and

lights and wash separately in tepid water either by hand or in the machine. It is not necessary to use soap powder but if you do it must be non-biological. If you prefer to work with new, unwashed fabrics, they should be tested for colour-fastness: cut a small square from each fabric and wash as described above.

To prevent fabric from fraying and tangling while being washed, snip a small triangle off all four corners. This will also tell you which fabrics have been washed once they are replaced on your shelves.

To stop colours from bleeding add ¼ cup salt to the last rinse water and let the fabric soak for 15 minutes. Another method is to soak the fabric in a solution of 3 parts cold water to 1 part white vinegar. If the fabric still bleeds - do not use it or ensure that the finished quilt is dry-cleaned.

FABRIC REQUIREMENTS

O nce you have decided on your block design, the next question is how much fabric will you need? Using our worksheet (see pages 102 to 111) and taking it step by step, this is not difficult to calculate and if you keep worksheets for all the quilts you make, you will have an excellent reference source for future quilts.

1 Size of bed quilt. Certain things have to be taken into consideration: what size is the mattress and should the sides of the quilt fall to the floor, or just to the valance, or just cover the top of the mattress? As a general guideline mattress sizes are as follows:

Cot	22 x 45 in (55 x 115 cm)
Twin	36 x 72 in (90 x 180 cm)
Double	54 x 72 in (135 x 180 cm)
King	60 x 78 in (150 x 200 cm)

Add to this measurement the amount you would like to hang over each side and the amount at top and bottom. Common quilt sizes are:

Cot	24 x 36 in (60 x 90 cm)
Twin	60 x 92 in (150 x 235 cm)
Double	80 x 96 in (205 x 245 cm)
King	102 x 102 in (260 x 260 cm)

2 Block size. This will depend on the size of the quilt you are making. You can always add borders and sashing to adjust the size of a quilt if necessary. A 6 in or 8 in (15 or 20 cm) block is a good size for a cot quilt but a 10 in or 12 in (25 or 30 cm) block would look better on a larger quilt.

3 Number of blocks. Multiply the number of blocks required across the quilt by the number of blocks down to achieve the required size before borders are added.

4 Fabrics per block. Refer to your block diagram and count the number of pieces in *each different fabric* and list.

Example:

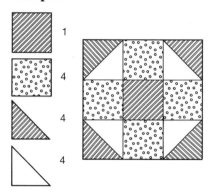

5 Fabrics per quilt. Multiply the number of pieces in each different fabric per block by the number of blocks and you have the total number of pieces per fabric required for the quilt.

6 Width of fabric. Most cotton fabrics are 44/45 in (112/113 cm) wide but do remember that they can shrink up to 5% when washed, so all calculations should take this into account. Our calculations are all based on 42 in (106 cm) wide fabric.

7 Number of templates per width. Divide the width of the fabric by the width of the template (don't forget the template must include the seam allowance).

Example: If you require a 4 in finished square, then divide 42 in (width of fabric)

by 4½ in (template witdh + ¼ in seam allowance all round). Answer = 9.3. Round this down to the nearest whole number and you now know that you can get nine 4½ in squares across the fabric width.

Or in metric: for a 10 cm finished square, divide 106 cm by 11 cm = 9.6, rounded down to 9.

8 Number of fabric strips. You have already calculated the number of pieces you need to cut, so divide this figure by 9 to get the number of fabric strips required.

Example: If you require 270 pieces you will need 30 fabric strips.

9 The height of your template determines the depth of the strip. For the 4½ in (11 cm) square the depth of the strip will be 4½ in (11 cm).

Example: To give 270 4½ in squares you need 30 x 4½ in = 135 in = 3¾ yards.

Or in metric: 30 x 11 cm = 3.30 metres. Now you know how to calculate the fabric amount for any regular pieced quilt.

HELPFUL FABRIC CALCULATION

The following charts will provide a ready calculator for working out fabric amounts when you are using the more common shapes and sizes for your templates. They record the number of templates which can be cut from five different lengths of fabric. The arrows on the template diagrams for each chart show the finished size and this is listed in the charts. However the number of templates includes a ¼ in (5 mm) seam allowance in each case.

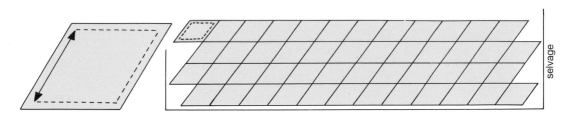

Number of 45° diamonds from 44 in (112 cm) width fabric

Finished size	8 in (20 cm)	16 in (40 cm)	24 in (60 cm)	32 in (80 cm)	39 in (1 m)
1 in (2.5 cm)	115	276	414	552	690
1½ in (4 cm)	72	144	234	306	378
2 in (5 cm)	42	98	154	210	266
2½ in (6 cm)	24	72	108	144	180
3 in (7.5 cm)	20	50	80	110	130
3½ in (9 cm)	18	45	63	90	108
4 in (10 cm)	16	32	48	64	80

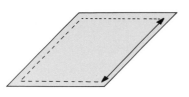
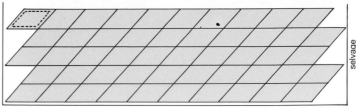

Number of 60° diamonds from 44 in (112 cm) width fabric

Finished size	8 in (20 cm)	16 in (40 cm)	24 in (60 cm)	32 in (80 cm)	39 in (1 m)
1 in (2.5 cm)	92	230	345	460	575
1½ in (4 cm)	54	126	198	270	342
2 in (5 cm)	28	84	126	168	210
2½ in (6 cm)	26	65	104	143	156
3 in (7.5 cm)	20	40	70	90	110
3½ in (9 cm)	9	36	54	72	90
4 in (10 cm)	8	24	40	56	72

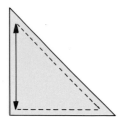
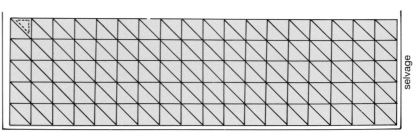

Number of right-angled triangles from 44 in (112 cm) width fabric

Finished size	8 in (20 cm)	16 in (40 cm)	24 in (60 cm)	32 in (80 cm)	39 in (1 m)
1 in (2.5 cm)	126	294	462	630	756
1½ in (4 cm)	68	204	306	408	510
2 in (5 cm)	56	140	196	280	336
2½ in (6 cm)	48	96	144	192	240
3 in (7.5 cm)	20	60	100	140	180
3½ in (9 cm)	18	54	90	108	144
4 in (10 cm)	16	48	64	96	112
4½ in (11.5 cm)	14	28	56	70	84
5 in (12.5 cm)	14	28	42	70	84

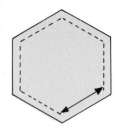

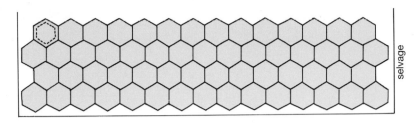

Number of hexagons from 44 in (112 cm) width fabric

Finished size	8 in (20 cm)	16 in (40 cm)	24 in (60 cm)	32 in (80 cm)	39 in (1 m)
¹/₂ in (1.5 cm)	108	243	378	378	594
³/₄ in (2 cm)	69	161	253	345	414
1 in (2.5 cm)	36	108	162	216	270
1¹/₂ in (4 cm)	12	48	72	96	120
2 in (5 cm)	10	30	50	70	80
2¹/₂ in (6 cm)	8	16	32	40	56
3 in (9 cm)	7	14	21	28	42

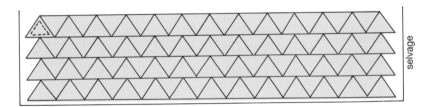

Number of equilateral triangles from 44 in (112 cm) width fabric

Finished size	8 in (20 cm)	16 in (40 cm)	24 in (60 cm)	32 in (80 cm)	39 in (1 m)
1 in (2.5 cm)	168	336	546	714	882
1¹/₂ in (4 cm)	102	204	340	442	544
2 in (5 cm)	56	140	224	308	364
2¹/₂ in (6 cm)	48	120	168	240	288
3 in (7.5 cm)	42	84	126	168	210
3¹/₂ in (9 cm)	19	76	114	152	190
4 in (10 cm)	17	51	85	102	136
4¹/₂ in (11.5 cm)	15	45	75	90	120
5 in (12.5 cm)	14	28	56	70	98

Number of squares from 44 in (112 cm) width fabric

Finished size	8 in (20 cm)	16 in (40 cm)	24 in (60 cm)	32 in (80 cm)	39 in (1 m)
1 in (2.5 cm)	140	280	420	560	700
1½ in (4 cm)	63	147	231	315	378
2 in (5 cm)	34	102	153	204	255
2½ in (6 cm)	28	70	98	140	168
3 in (7.5 cm)	24	48	72	96	120
3½ in (9 cm)	10	30	50	70	90
4 in (10 cm)	9	27	45	54	72
4½ in (11.5 cm)	8	24	32	48	56
5 in (12.5 cm)	7	14	28	35	42
5½ in (14 cm)	7	14	21	35	42
6 in (15 cm)	6	12	18	24	30

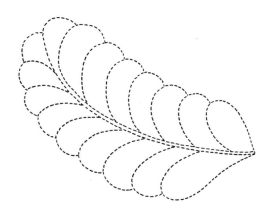

NOTES

DRAFTING TEMPLATES

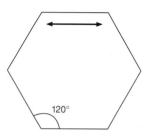

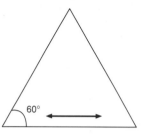

Hexagon Six-sided shape with 120° angles. All sides are equal.

Equilateral triangle Three-sided shape with 60° angles. All sides are equal.

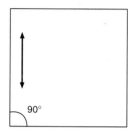

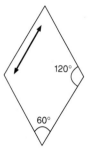

Square Four-sided shape with 90° angles. All sides are equal.

Diamond Four-sided shape with two 60° and two 120° angles. All sides are equal. Six of these together form the six-pointed star.

Rectangle Four-sided shape with two sets of parallel sides. All angles are 90°.

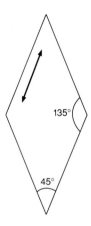

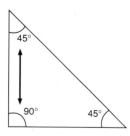

Right-angled triangle Half a square with one 90° angle and two 45° angles.

Long diamond Four-sided shape with two 45° angles and two 135° angles. All sides are equal. Eight of these form an eight-pointed star.

30

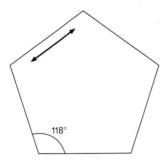

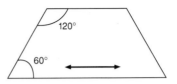

Pentagon Five-sided shape with 108° angles. All sides are equal.

Half-hexagon Four-sided shape with two 120° and two 60° angles.

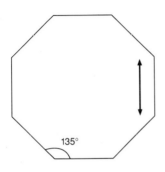

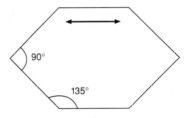

Long hexagon (or Church Window) Six sides of equal length, four angles of 135° and two of 90°.

Octagon Eight-sided shape with 135° angles. It must be worked with a square of the same size as one of the sides.

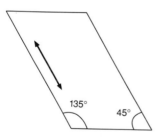

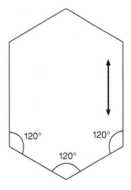

Rhomboid A shape formed from two irregular triangles, with two sets of parallel sides. The finer angle is 45° and the wider 135°.

Elongated hexagon (or Coffin) Two long sides of equal length and four short sides of equal length. All angles are 120°.

DRAFTING AMERICAN BLOCKS

Most American blocks are drafted on a grid system. An understanding of the grid system will enable you to see and draft the individual shapes contained in most quilt blocks. The most common grids are the "four patch" which is made up of 4 squares; the "nine patch" (9 squares); the "five patch" (25 squares) and the "seven patch" (49 squares).

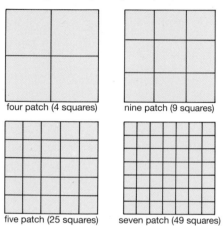

four patch (4 squares)   nine patch (9 squares)

five patch (25 squares)   seven patch (49 squares)

2   Find the next number on an imperial measurement ruler, higher than 12, that can be divided evenly by 5, i.e. 15. Place the zero of the ruler on the bottom left-hand corner of the square and place the 15 in mark on the ruler on the right hand side.
3   Since 15 in divided by 5 is 3, mark the paper with a dot every 3 in, i.e. at 3 in, 6 in, 9 in and 12 in.
4   Mark vertical lines through the four dots, parallel to the sides of the square.
5   Turn the paper 90° and repeat the procedure.

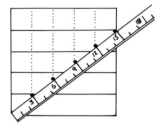

Marking a grid is normally a simple process, e.g. a 12 in block divides easily into a "nine patch". Each square on the grid will measure 4 in. If using metric measurements a basic block would be 30 cm wide, as this divides easily into 2, 3 and 5. To divide a 30 cm block into 7, see below.

Dividing a 12 in block into a "five patch"

There are times, however, when a block will not divide so easily, for example when you want to divide a 12 in square into fifths for a "five patch". Work as follows:
1   Draw a 12 in square on plain paper.

Depending on the size of your block it might be necessary to work in $\frac{1}{2}$ in or $1\frac{1}{2}$ in increments. For example, when dividing a 9 in square into a "seven patch" you would find that the measurement higher than 9 which is divisible by 7 is 14 in and this would go off the edge of your square, so use $1\frac{1}{2}$ in increments. Place the $10\frac{1}{2}$ in mark of the ruler on the edge of the square and mark the paper with a dot every $1\frac{1}{2}$ in.

Dividing a 30 cm block into a "seven patch"

Follow the same method for a 30 cm metric square as above. The nearest number which can be easily divided by 7 is 35.

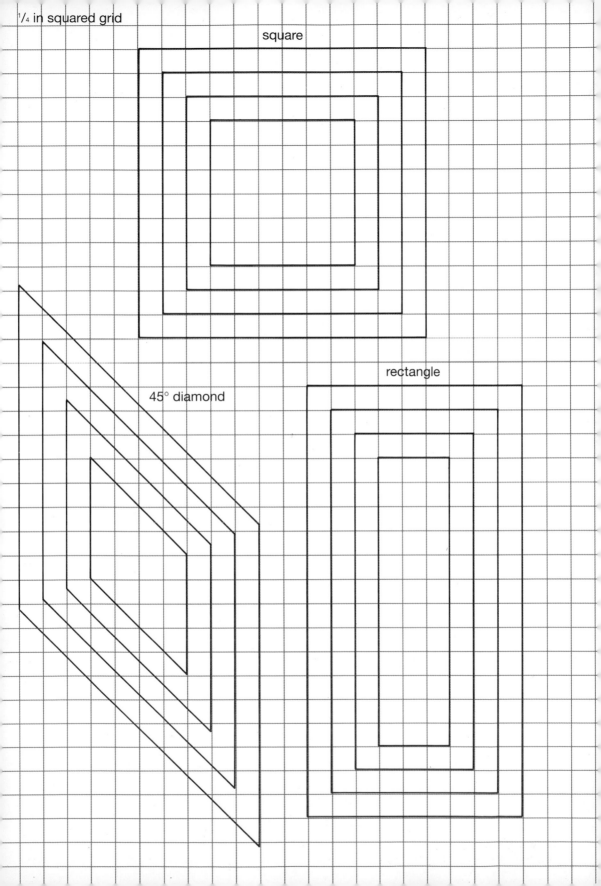

¼ in isometric grid

hexagon

elongated hexagon

equilateral triangle

60° diamond

half hexagon

¹/₄ in isometric grid

¼ in isometric grid

5mm isometric grid

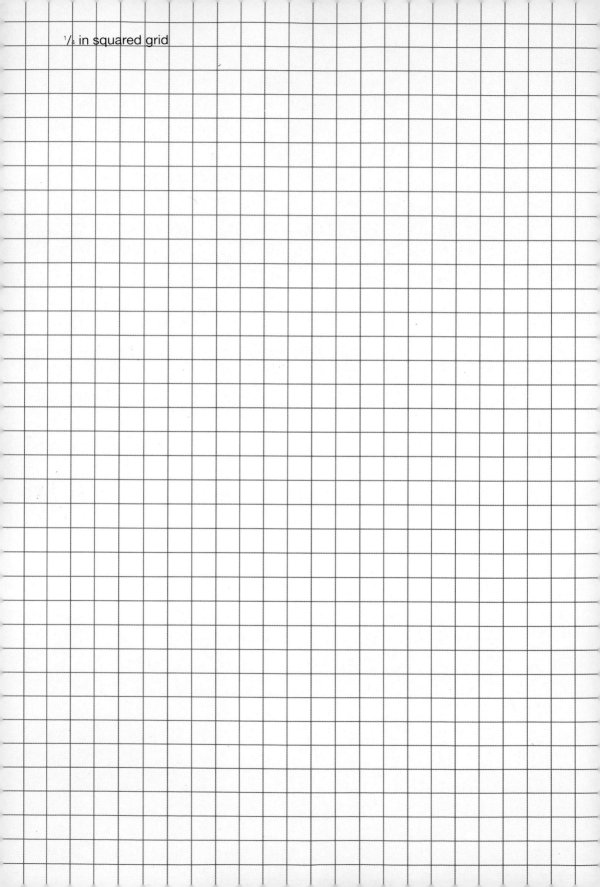

¹/₄ in squared grid

5mm squared grid

These blocks are very simply pieced and therefore ideal for beginners.

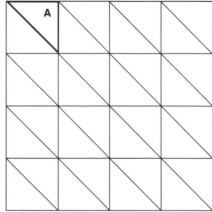

LOG CABIN TRIANGLES

The design of this block which is made solely from one triangle template, is formed from separating the light and dark fabrics.

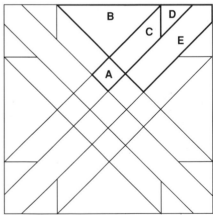

MEXICAN STAR

This block is more easily pieced diagonally.

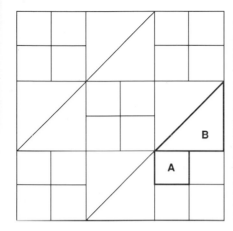

JACOB'S LADDER

Always a favourite block. For variation, substitute a nine-patch square for the four-patch.

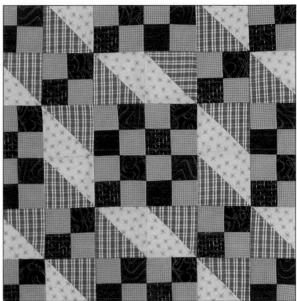

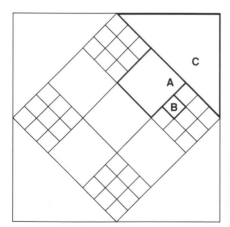

DOUBLE NINE-PATCH

The simple nine-patch can be used in endless ways. Often seen in antique Amish quilts. Enhanced here by setting on point.

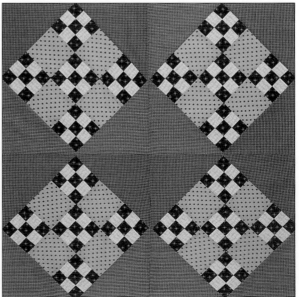

47

These blocks can be speedily cut and stitched using the rotary cutter and sewing machine. No templates are required.

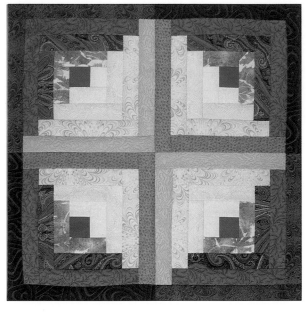

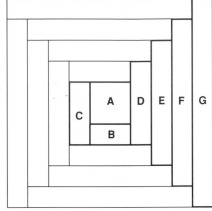

LOG CABIN

Traditionally the centre square is red representing the hearth fire. One side of the block uses dark fabrics and the other light.

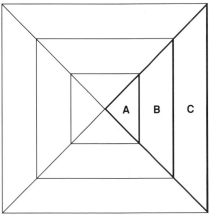

MITRED SQUARE

Three strips of equal width are joined together, then cut into triangles.

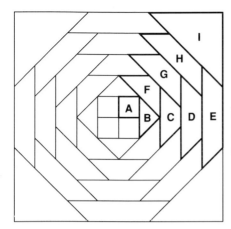

PINEAPPLE

This is a variation of Log Cabin. Looks equally effective using pastels or strong Amish colours.

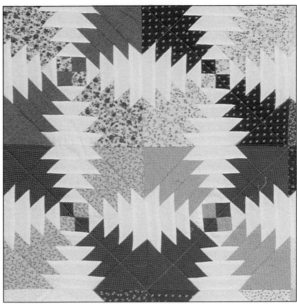

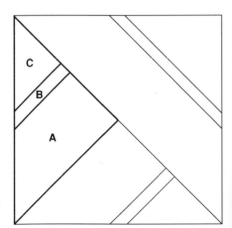

WINDMILL BLADES

Six strips of various widths are joined together and cut into triangles to form two blocks.

These blocks have straight seams but give the illusion of curves when pieced.

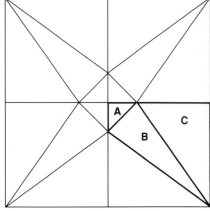

CROSSED CANOES
Also called 'Tippecanoe'. Looks effective in just two fabrics but more could be used.

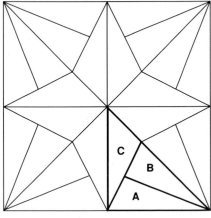

BLAZING STAR
Also called 'Mother's Delight'. Needs care when piecing but well worth the effort.

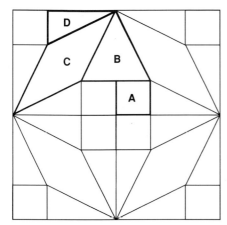

SPARKLING JEWEL

Much easier to piece than it looks. Sew template B to central four-patch, then add template C and the corner units already pieced.

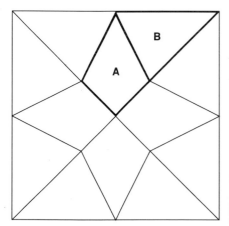

SNOWFLAKE

Very simply pieced. Would look great as a scrap quilt and the background could be used to show off some fine hand quilting.

As on the previous two pages, these blocks are
made up of straight lines which appear curved when
joined together.

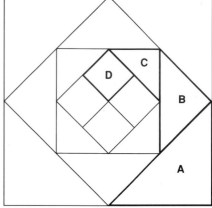

SNAIL'S TRAIL
Often called 'Indiana puzzle' and always
looks effective. Try with alternate plain
blocks in both of the colours.

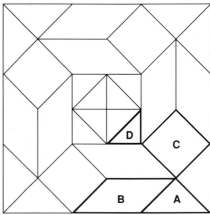

ROUGH SEA
The three-dimensional effect can be
changed by different placement of the
light, medium and dark fabrics.

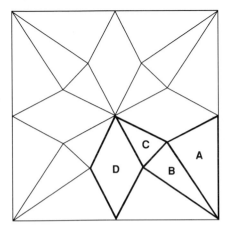

NORTH STAR

Easily pieced by forming central star, then adding corner units.

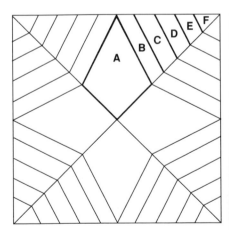

STRING BLOCK

The strips in this block can be cut using the 45° Kaleidoscope ruler as shown on page 13.

The piecing of these blocks can be simplified by partial seaming. This is when the first seam is left incomplete until the rest of the surround is stitched.

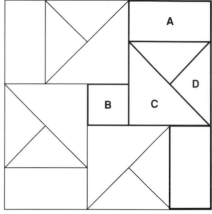

CHASING TAILS

Join templates A, C and D into units and stitch around template B.

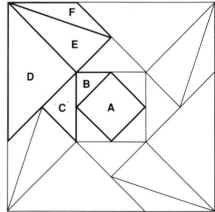

ECCENTRIC STAR

This can be pieced easily by joining templates D, E and F into units, then stitching them around the square formed by templates A, B and C.

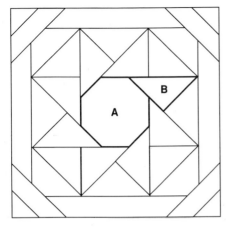

TWISTED STAR

The twisted star is enhanced by pineapple strips, which create an interesting secondary design when the blocks are joined together.

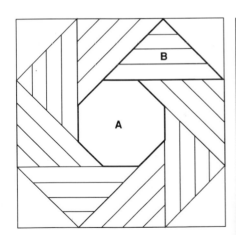

BASKET WEAVE

Simple to piece but it does need sashing between the blocks. Make the striped triangles by sewing long strips together then cutting to template B.

These blocks all have gentle curves and are
therefore suitable for machine as well as hand
piecing.

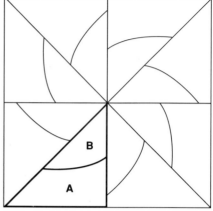

ROTATING PINWHEEL
A very popular block in the 1930s when
it was pieced with bright colours on a
calico background.

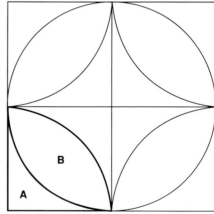

ORANGE PEEL
Try making this just with scrap fabrics
not only for the peel segments but also
for the background.

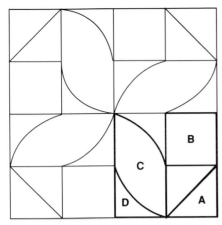

WINDFLOWER

The look of this block can be totally changed by using strong Amish colours.

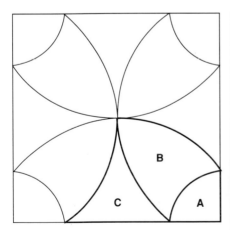

WINDING WAYS

This also looks very effective if pieced using just two colours for the whole quilt.

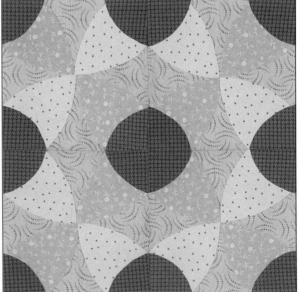

Each of these blocks has been made using just two fabrics. Reversing the colours on alternate blocks makes a simple but effective quilt.

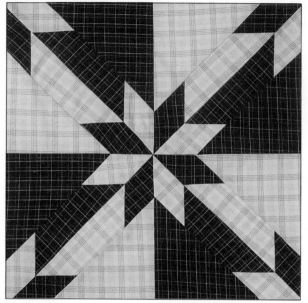

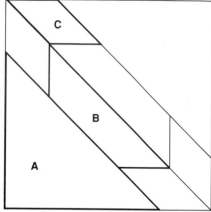

HUNTER'S STAR

When looking at this block as a single unit you do not immediately see the star, which becomes obvious when the blocks are joined.

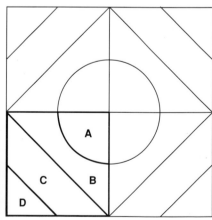

NOUGHTS & CROSSES

This block has a nice combination of straight and curved lines and looks effective in pastels.

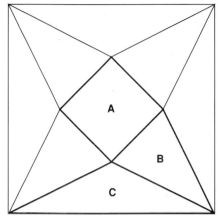

WORLD WITHOUT END

This block looks great with template B formed from brightly coloured strips of fabric and templates A and C in black.

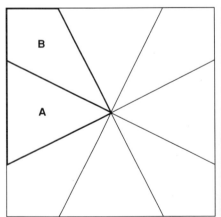

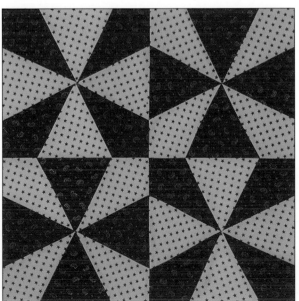

LIGHT & SHADOW

If you are feeling adventurous with colour, try graduating the depth of colour from one diagonal point of the quilt to another.

A series of ingeniously overlapping templates makes
these particularly effective.

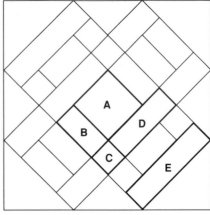

DOUBLE LINKS
Easier when pieced on the diagonal with
squares and rectangles, although it can
be pieced with half and quarter-square
triangles.

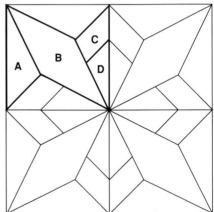

BARBARA BANNISTER STAR
The choice of fabric will determine how
much of the square will recede into the
background.

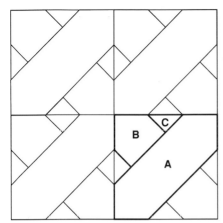

KENTUCKY CHAIN

Try this block cutting the various stripes from one border fabric.

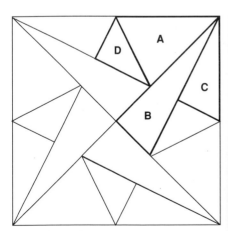

STARRY PATH

A good block to use up scraps set against a calico backing.

The half-rectangle can easily be pieced using the Bi-Rangle (see page 13). These complex looking blocks give the illusion of curves.

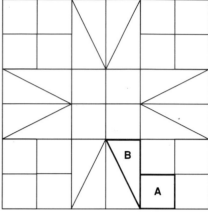

BIRD OF PARADISE
Simply pieced using half-rectangles with a four-patch.

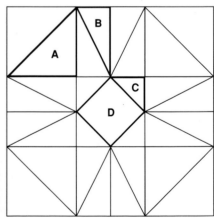

DORIS'S DELIGHT
Why not use this interesting block for an Album Quilt, signing your name in the centre square?

WESTERN STAR

This block does contain a great number of pieces but the result is very rewarding.

A selection of blocks suitable for using up scraps.

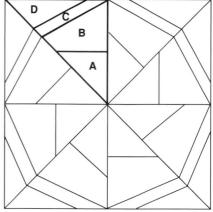

WHEEL OF FORTUNE
Looks good with calico but can look very dramatic with primary colours on black.

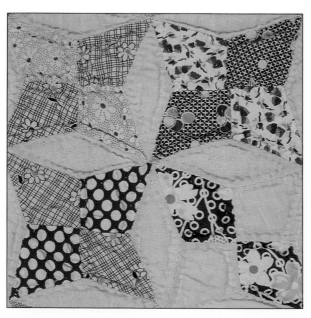

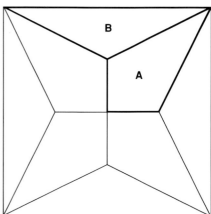

FOUR POINTED STAR
Easily pieced and looks better when the block is no more than 8 in (20 cm) square.

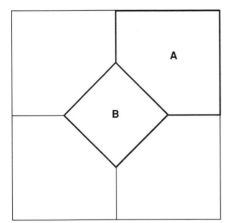

BOW TIE

A more sophisticated quilt can be obtained by making the bow ties from varying shades of the same colour.

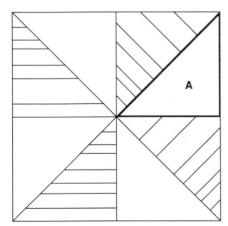

STRIP TRIANGLE

The pieced triangles are a wonderful way of using up your tiny scraps.

NOTES

NOTES

NOTES

NOTES

HAND PIECING

English patchwork

This method of patchwork can be used for any design but it is especially good for piecing intricate shapes such as the hexagon and diamond. The basis of this technique is that fabric shapes are sewn over paper templates. These paper templates must be accurately cut - they must be the exact size and shape of the finished patch.

1   Either buy or make a master template the size of the required patch without seam allowance. Some popular shapes in common sizes are given on pages 33 to 35. The template has to be used many times, so if you are making your own, use plastic: cardboard is just not durable enough.

2   One paper template has to be made for every patch. Any paper will do – typing paper is a good weight. Draw round your master template carefully and cut out accurately along the pencil line. Keeping these paper templates accurate is the secret of success.

3   Pin the paper templates to the wrong side of the fabric allowing space for seam allowances and trying to keep two opposite sides of your shape on the straight of the grain. Cut out approximately $1/4$ in (5 mm) all round for the seam allowance. This does not have to be absolutely accurate – it can be judged by eye.

4   Turn the seam allowance over the edge of the paper, folding the corners carefully, and tack in place. Sew right through fabric and paper with a contrasting thread, so

that it can be seen easily for removal later. Press the patches as this helps them to lie flat and helps keep the corners sharp.

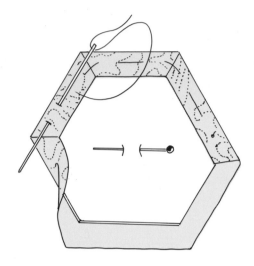

5   To join the patches, place them right sides together and oversew the seam in a matching thread as neatly as possible.

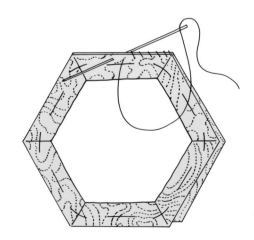

6   When all the patches are sewn together, remove the tacking thread and papers.

American block piecing

Templates for each different shape in the chosen block must be made, preferably out of plastic. These templates must include a ¼ in (5 mm) seam allowance all round. The details which follow are based on the "Shoo-Fly" block.

1   Lay the fabric out flat, wrong side up. Place the template on the fabric making sure as many edges as possible are on the straight of the grain.

2   Draw round the template carefully with a marking pencil. Extreme care must be taken as accuracy here is very important. Cut out on the marked lines.

3   On the wrong side of the fabric mark the stitching line ¼ in (5 mm) from the cut edge using a ¼ in (5 mm) marker.

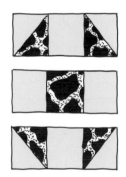

4   As a general rule the smallest patches are sewn together first. This would be the triangles in "Shoo-Fly". Place two pieces right sides together and, starting at the beginning of the marked sewing line, take two small back stitches. Continue across the line with small running stitches, checking every so often to see that the marked line on the front is lined up with the marked line of the back piece. When you reach the end of the marked sewing line take two more back stitches. Never stitch into the seam allowance. Cut the thread. Press the seams towards the darker fabric after each new patch is joined.

5   Sew these units together in rows, then join the rows together to form blocks.

ROTARY CUTTING AND MACHINE PIECING

The rotary cutter speeds up the cutting process so that, coupled with machine piecing, patchwork quilts really can be made accurately and efficiently in a fraction of the time it takes to hand stitch them. There is no need for templates and no need for marking sewing and cutting lines on your fabric. Accuracy, however, is of the utmost importance and care must be taken in checking measurements before cutting. The fabric is cut in two stages, firstly into strips across the width and secondly into patches. You will need rotary cutter, ruler and cutting mat (see page 13).

Cutting strips

1   Before cutting with a rotary cutter the edge of the fabric must be straightened. Fold the fabric in half, selvage to selvage, then fold again, aligning the folded edge with the selvages. Place the ruler across the fabric so that one of the perpendicular lines marked on it is aligned with the double fold of the fabric. Hold the ruler firmly with your left hand and the cutter in the right. Keeping the blade against the edge of the ruler, push the cutter *away* from the body in one even movement (see diagram).

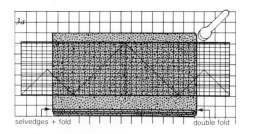

Left-handed people should reverse these instructions but the important thing is always to cut away from the body.

2   Rotate the cutting mat so that the ruler can still be held firmly with the left hand, and you are now ready to cut strips, moving from left to right across the fabric (see diagram). Check every so often that the fabric is still straight by opening up a strip. If the cuts are not perpendicular to the fold, the strips, when opened, will form a shallow zigzag, and you will need to repeat step 1 to re-straighten the edge.

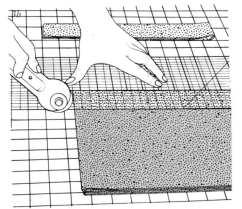

Cutting squares or rectangles

1   Cut a strip to the required finished width of the square or rectangle plus ½ in (1 cm) for seam allowances. Leave it folded.

2   Trim off the selvage/fold edge. Working across from this cut edge, cut the strips into the desired length of square or rectangle, adding ½ in (1 cm) seam allowance. Depending on the size of square or rectangle, it is sometimes necessary to unfold the double-fold edge to obtain 2 extra squares or rectangles.

Cutting half-square triangles

These triangles are half of a square with the two short sides on the straight of the grain of the fabric and the long side on the bias. To cut these triangles cut a square $^7/_8$ in (1.7 cm) larger than the finished size of the square formed from pieced triangles, e.g. if the finished size is 4 in (10 cm), cut a square measuring $4^7/_8$ in (11.7 cm). Then cut this in half diagonally.

Quarter-square triangles

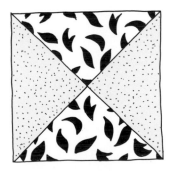

These triangles have their short sides on the bias and the long side on the straight of the grain. They are formed from a square cut $1^1/_4$ in (2.4 cm) larger than the finished size of the pieced square, e.g. for finished size 4 in (10 cm) cut a square $5^1/_4$ in (12.4 cm) and then cut the square diagonally both ways into four triangles.

Chain piecing

Chain piecing is the technique of feeding a series of pieces through the sewing machine without lifting the presser foot and without cutting the thread between each piece. Always chain piece when you can - it saves time and thread.

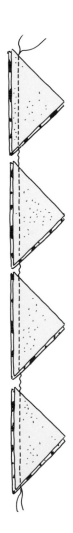

SQUARES AND TRIANGLES

Many interesting designs can be produced just by using squares, half-square triangles and quarter-square triangles. You could spend a lifetime using only these shapes and you still wouldn't run out of variations. Here are just a few to give you some ideas. When cutting these squares and triangles to include the seam allowance just remember the magic formulae and you will end up with the correct finished size:

1   Cut squares $1/2$ in (1 cm) larger.
2   Cut half-square triangles $7/8$ in (1.7 cm) larger.
3   Cut quarter-square triangles $1^1/4$ in (2.4 cm) larger.

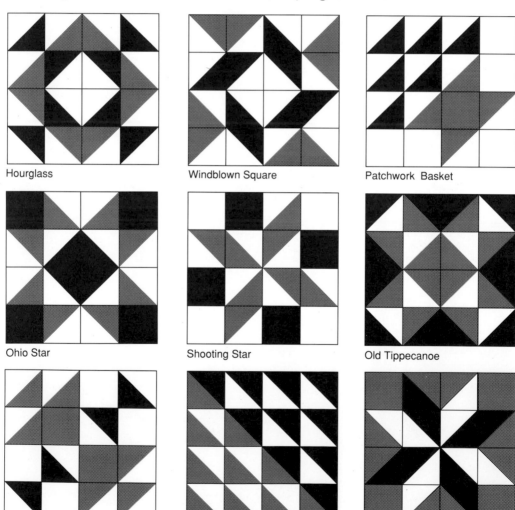

Hourglass	Windblown Square	Patchwork Basket
Ohio Star	Shooting Star	Old Tippecanoe
Old Maid's Puzzle	Flying Geese	Evening Star

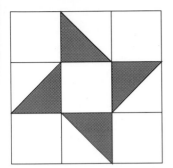

Friendship Star

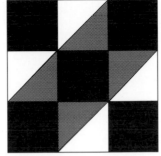

Country Garden

Shoofly

Double X Variation

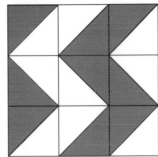

Chevron

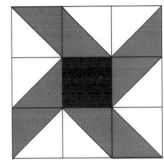

Formal Garden

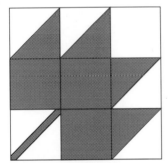

Maple Leaf

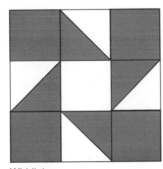

Whirligig

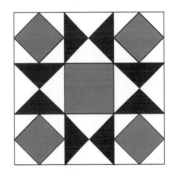

Combination Star

Yankee Puzzle

Marions Choice

Texas Star

DIAGONALLY DIVIDED BLOCKS

Some blocks are made up of pieces which form a diagonal line across the block. By using light fabrics in one half and dark in the other or two contrasting colours in either half, lots of interesting secondary designs for the overall quilt emerge. The most famous diagonally divided block is the Log Cabin (page 48) which usually has one light half

and one dark half and a red square representing the hearth fire in the centre. It is not by any means the only block which can be divided diagonally (see "Log Cabin Triangles" on page 46, for example). Below are a few ideas for creating overall quilt designs using log cabin or other diagonally divided blocks.

NOTES

NOTES

NOTES

NOTES

CALCULATING SASHING REQUIREMENTS

If you are sashing a quilt and do not want to have sashing squares, it is preferable to have either the widthwise or the lengthwise sashing in one piece. You will usually have sufficient fabric if you measure across the width of the quilt and buy this length of fabric but there are times, depending on the ratio between the number of blocks and the size of the sashing, when this is not sufficient. If you haven't calculated exactly — buy the lengthwise measurement which is:

(No. of blocks down x block size) + (No. of widthwise sashing strips x width of sashing)

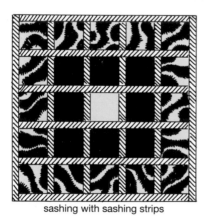

sashing with sashing strips

For most size quilts it is more economical to use sashing squares since you only need strips of fabric the length of your block plus seam allowance. This can normally be juggled out of less fabric as you don't need to buy any long lengths. There is an easy formula for calculating how many strips you need to go with the squares:

(No. of blocks across x [No. of blocks down + 1]) + (No. of blocks down x [No. of blocks across + 1])

The strips should be the width of your sashing plus seam allowance.

To calculate how much fabric you will need, divide the width of your fabric by the length of block plus seam allowance. For example you would get 3 sashing strips for a 12 in block (12½ in with seam allowance) from a 45 in wide fabric. For a 30 cm block (31 cm with seam allowance), you would get three strips from 114 cm wide fabric. However many sashing strips you require in total should then be divided by this number, which will give you the number of widthwise strips you need to cut from your fabric. It is then a simple calculation to multiply this number by the width of sashing required plus seam allowance. This gives the total amount of fabric to buy.

sashing with sashing squares

Sashing squares

To calculate how many sashing squares you need to cut:

(No. of blocks down + 1) x (No. of blocks across + 1)

These squares should be cut the width of sashing required plus seam allowance.

TIPS FOR SETTING ON POINT

A block can take on a totally new look when set diagonally or "on point". When planning a quilt set diagonally there are a few points to take into consideration:

1   In order to calculate the measurements of your quilt you need to know the measurement of the block from point to point. To calculate this you multiply the size of the finished block by 1.414.
Example: A 12 in (30 cm) block will measure 16.97 in or just under 17 in (42.42 or nearly 42.5 cm).
Now you can calculate how many blocks you require for your quilt size.

2   Piece rows diagonally, starting at a corner. Triangles have to be added to the end of each row *before* joining rows and these are called "setting triangles".

3   Setting triangles form the outside of your quilt and should not be on the bias. To ensure this, these triangles should be formed from *quarter-square triangles*, i.e. a

square cut into four (see page 73). This square is the diagonal measurement of your block plus 1¼ in (2.4 cm) for seam allowance. Therefore for a 12 in block (diagonal measurement approximately 17 in) the square should be 18¼ in. A 30 cm (42.5 cm diagonally) block needs a 44.9 cm square.

4   Add the four corners last. Again the outside edges of your quilt should not be on the bias and to ensure this these corners are cut from *half-square triangles* (see page 73). To calculate the size, divide the finished size of your block by 1.414, then add ⅞ in (1.7 cm) for seam allowance.
Example: 12 in divided by 1.414 = 8.49 in + ⅞ in (0.875 in) = 9.37 in (or 9½ in, as it can be trimmed later).
Or in metric: 30 cm ÷ 1.414 = 21.22 cm + 1.7 cm = 22.9 cm (or 23 cm).

APPLIQUÉ

Appliqué is the art of applying one fabric on top of another as opposed to patchwork in which pieces are stitched together. Appliqué quilts are often pictorial since the technique lends itself to smaller and more intricate designs.

Traditionally these quilts are sewn by hand. Nowadays, however, appliquéd quilts are often machine sewn with a close satin stitch using the wide variety of shaded, metallic and rayon threads that are now available.

Hand Appliqué

There are several methods of hand appliqué but the principle is the same. The appliqué pieces are cut with a seam allowance. This

This appliqué Baltimore sampler quilt is made in traditional reds and greens.

is turned under and the piece is sewn to the background fabric using a fine thread to match the colour of the appliqué fabric. A small invisible hemming stitch is used from the fold of the appliqué straight down into the background and returning to the fold 1/8-1/4 in (3-5 mm) further on.

Machine Appliqué

The appliqué shapes are cut without a seam allowance, then either pinned or glued in position. The sewing machine is set for a close, small zig-zag stitch and an appropriate foot fitted – clear if possible.

When satin stitching around shapes, the entire stitch width should be on the appliqué, so that when the needle is in the right hand position it is just off the edge of the appliqué.

To go around intricate shapes you must pivot the needle, i.e. leave the needle in the fabric, lift the foot and move the fabric. On concave shapes the needle is left on the appliqué shape. On convex shapes the needle is left on the background. Two or three pivots may be necessary on tight bends.

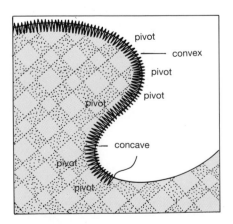

TYPES OF APPLIQUÉ

Bias Appliqué (Stained Glass Appliqué) The designs of stained glass windows can be adapted to fabric by placing pieces of fabric, usually plain coloured, in a planned design, on a backing fabric. The raw edges of the fabrics are covered with black bias binding which suggests the lead used in stained glass.

Celtic Appliqué Another way of using bias binding is in Celtic appliqué which features traditional Celtic patterns. These designs, normally symmetrical, are drawn on a backing fabric and the bias binding is then placed on top of the lines and is woven under and over itself following the intricate patterns.

Broderie Perse This form of appliqué dates back to the seventeenth century. Motifs of flowers, birds and trees from printed fabric are cut out and placed on a background fabric to create a new design. They often form the central motif for a medallion quilt and can be either hand or machine appliquéd.

Hawaiian Appliqué Quilting was taken to Hawaii by the early missionaries and it is said that their individual quiltmaking came about due to the lack of any scrap fabric on the island - the locals did not wear clothes! Two layers of solid fabric are used for each quilt - one is left whole and forms the background fabric while the other is folded, then cut, to create symmetrical designs usually representing the luxurious flowers on the island. This is opened out, placed over the background fabric and all raw edges turned under and stitched to the fabric beneath. A distinctive feature of these quilts is the close-set quilting lines which echo the design of the central motif.

Reverse Appliqué This is a decorative form of appliqué particularly used by Central and South American Indians. Two or more layers of fabric are placed on top of each other, then the design is cut away from the top layer or layers revealing the different fabrics beneath. The raw edges are turned under and sewn invisibly to the layer below.

Shadow Appliqué A layer of sheer or transparent fabric is placed on top of a brightly coloured appliqué design to create a subtle, shadowy effect. The layers are held together with quilting stitches worked around the edge of the appliqué.

QUILTING

A quilt is made up of three layers – the backing, the wadding and the quilt top. These three layers are tacked together, then quilted.

Backing This can be a printed or a plain fabric or a simply pieced patchwork – remember your quilt will be reversible. Quilting stitches will show up more on a plain fabric. For this reason a beginner might prefer a printed fabric. The backing fabric should be at least 2 in (5 cm) larger all around than the quilt top.

Wadding A 2oz (70g) polyester wadding is recommended for hand quilting. This is roughly equivalent to the low-loft batting available in the United States. American quilters also have a choice of thinner, more solid battings, such as needle-punched polyester and bonded cotton batting which create a flatter finish. In Britain polyester wadding comes in several thicknesses and in white or charcoal grey but the thicker wadding is only suitable for tied quilts. Pure cotton wadding is also available but this needs to be heavily quilted (every 1 in/2.5 cm) to keep it from bunching up when washed. Polyfelt wadding produces a flatter finish suitable for wallhangings and quilted clothing but this will also need to be heavily quilted. The wadding should also be 2 in (5 cm) larger all around than the quilt top.

Quilt top If you need to mark a quilting design on your top this must be done before joining the three layers. Quilting designs can be taken from numerous books or stencils. Some popular designs are given on pages 91 to 92. They have been drawn on a grid for ease of enlargement, although this can, of course, be easily done on a photocopier. Transfer the design to the right side of the fabric. The easiest way to do this is to trace it straight onto the fabric. If the fabric is dark you will need a light source beneath it. Simple quilting designs can be made by using any curved or straight objects. Masking tape is useful for marking straight lines and the same piece of tape can be lifted and used several times. There are many marker pens and pencils available but whatever you decide to use, it is very important to test it first to ensure it will not permanently mark the fabric. The water erasable markers are popular but remember to remove marks before pressing as this can set the lines. The silver, yellow and white marking pencils are good, as is an ordinary hard lead pencil, but keep the point sharp and take care not to press too hard, the secret being to mark only as much as necessary to see the design.

How to join the layers Lay the backing fabric right side down, preferably on a smooth surface. Tape the corners to hold the fabric down flat. Lay the wadding on top, taking care to smooth out any wrinkles. Lay the quilt top right side up centrally on top. Tack the three layers together in a grid, starting in the centre and working out to the edges. The rows of tacking should be about 6 in (15 cm) apart. Alternatively, if machine quilting or tying, the three layers can be pin basted using 1 in (2.5 cm) safety pins, again every 6 in (15 cm). Avoid placing the pins on quilting lines.

A close-up detail from a wholecloth quilt made in the north of England in the early 1900s.

Hand Quilting

You will need quilting thread, betweens needles, small scissors and a thimble. You can quilt on a frame, in a quilting hoop or just in your lap. For best results a frame or hoop is recommended. Betweens needles are shorter and finer than ordinary needles. The shorter the needle, the smaller the stitch produced. It is traditional to choose a quilting thread to blend with the quilt top, although you may prefer to use a contrasting thread to show off your quilting design. Quilting thread is usually used as it is strong and will not knot as it is treated with beeswax.

The quilting stitch is a simple running stitch. It is more important to have straight stitches of equal length and spacing than to have tiny, uneven stitches. A good target to aim for is to have 10 stitches to 1 in (20 stitches to 5 cm). The stitches on the back should be the same size as those on the top. Start quilting in the centre of the quilt and work outwards.

1   To begin quilting, thread a needle with an 18 in (45 cm) length of quilting thread, knot it, and insert the needle from the top into the wadding a short distance from where you plan to start. Bring the needle out at the starting point. Tug lightly on the thread to pop the knot into the wadding. You are aiming to make it impossible to tell where the quilting line begins and ends.

2   Have a thimble on the middle finger of your right hand (reverse if you are left-handed). The hand with the thimble is your sewing hand and stays on top of the quilt, the other hand stays below the quilt. The index finger of this hand should also

be protected. Holding the needle perpendicular to the quilt or at a very slight angle, push it through the fabric with the top of the thimble until you can just feel the point with your left index finger. To bring the needle back to the top, press the eye of the needle flat against the quilt with the thimble while pushing the point of the needle up with your left index finger. With practice, you should be able to put several stitches on your needle before pulling it all the way through the fabric.

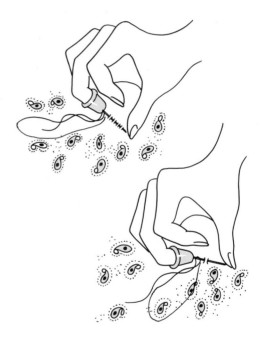

3   To end the quilting, tie a knot a short distance from your work, make a final stitch through the top and the wadding and out again a needle length or two away, then pull the knot through to the inside of the wadding and cut the thread.

Machine Quilting

Machine quilting is worth considering as it saves a great deal of time and also produces quilts that can withstand machine washing better than hand-quilted pieces.

Thread your bobbin with a good quality thread in a colour to match your backing. The top thread should match your quilt top. Alternatively an invisible nylon thread can be used, which will produce a softer effect.

Straight line quilting. Machine quilting is only successful if you have a walking foot or even feed foot, which will feed both the top and the bottom layers evenly through the machine. Place your machine on a large table so that the quilt is supported at the side and the back while it is being stitched.

Starting at one side, roll the quilt towards the centre up to the start of the quilting. Secure the roll tightly with bicycle clips to enable it to go neatly under the head of the machine. Quilt a central line from the top to the bottom of the quilt. Unroll the quilt to the next quilting line and quilt. Continue in this way, until you reach the edge, then roll from the opposite side and quilt in the same manner.

Free-motion quilting. This method allows you to stitch curved and intricate quilting patterns. Use a darning foot and drop the feed dogs so that you will be able to move the quilt in any direction without having to turn it. If you are new to free-motion quilting, an embroidery hoop is useful to keep the fabric flat and provide the right amount of fabric tension. Without the feed dogs the stitch length is controlled by how fast or how slowly you move the

quilt through the machine. The aim is to produce small, even stitches. Practise on a spare piece of fabric until you are happy with the result.

Tying

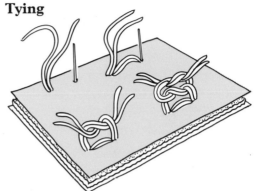

Tying is an excellent and quick alternative way of holding the layers of a quilt together and is especially useful if a very thick wadding has been used, which would be difficult to either hand or machine quilt.

To mark the placement of the ties, insert pins through all three layers, not more than 6 in (15 cm) apart. Thread your needle with a length of 6 strand embroidery thread in a contrasting colour. Push the needle through all three layers of quilt leaving approximately 4 in (10 cm) of thread either at the top or the bottom depending on whether you want your ties to be on the top or bottom of your quilt, and bring the needle back to where it entered. Go down and come up again through the same holes. Cut the thread leaving a second end of 4 in (10 cm). Tie the two ends together in a knot, right over left, then left over right. Snip the ends to the desired length. Space your knots evenly over the entire quilt top. For an alternative effect, very fine ribbon can be tied into bows.

TYPES OF QUILTING

Background Quilting fills large, often plain, areas with a regular pattern. The background of appliqué areas often has cross-grid quilting which not only makes the background recede but also gives a pleasing contrast to the appliqué curves.

Echo or Contour Quilting is normally used around Hawaiian appliqué designs. Several lines of quilting run parallel to the edge of the appliqué and at equally spaced distances from it.

In the Ditch quilting is used when you wish to add puffiness to a quilt but don't want quilting lines to add an extra element of design. The quilting stitches are placed in the seams. This form of quilting is usually done by machine as the stitches do not show.

Outline Quilting emphasizes the design and shapes of the patchwork top. The quilting stitches are worked ¼ in (5 mm) away from the seam lines of certain patches: ¼ in (5 mm) masking tape gives a perfect guide.

Sashiko is a form of Japanese quilting which is traditionally worked on indigo dyed cloth with thick white cotton thread. Long stitches are traditional in sashiko quilting, between five to seven stitches per inch (2.5 cm). The stitches are said to resemble rice grains.

Selective Quilting emphasizes the secondary design pieced blocks can give. For example in "World Without End" (page 59) the illusion of circles would be quilted and "Trip Around the World"

could be quilted across the squares to give the illusion of triangles. Remember that even though your patchwork top might only have straight lines, a curved quilting pattern could add extra dimensions. For example a "Log Cabin" design with arcs of quilting stitches can look fantastic.

Stippling is a technique in which the quilting stitches are randomly and densely placed to fill the background with texture. Because it also flattens the areas where it is worked, it has the effect of making the remaining parts appear puffier by contrast.

Trapunto and Corded Quilting (Italian) Both use a fine cotton for the top and a loosely woven fabric, such as muslin, for the back. Corded quilting has two parallel lines sewn by hand or machine to form the design and thick wool is threaded through the muslin and between the sewn channel to give a raised effect. Trapunto has a soft sculptured effect which is achieved by stuffing a design from the back with teased out wadding or wool.

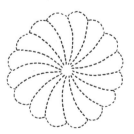

QUILT MOTIFS

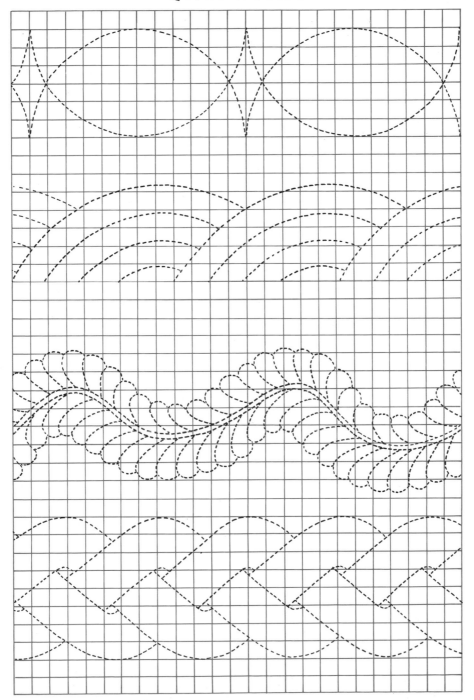

FINISHING A QUILT

Borders

Borders are extremely useful in that they can extend your quilt to the exact size required. They also frame the design effectively. They do, however, need to be in proportion to the quilt and if a very wide border is required, it is better to have two or three borders of varying widths than just one. Borders can be intricately pieced, plain with elaborate quilting or made from border fabric. The corners can be either straight or mitred.

Mitred borders Measure the length of the quilt as above but cut two border strips the length of the quilt plus twice the width of the border. Measure and cut the widthwise strips in the same manner.

Sew the border strips to the quilt as above but begin and end 1/4 in (5 mm) away from corners, backstitching either end.

With the quilt right side up, fold one border strip under itself at a 45° angle. Press and slipstitch in place. Trim the excess fabric. Repeat on the other corners.

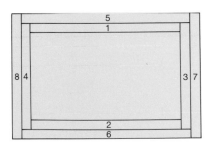

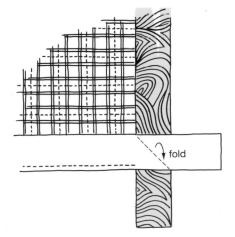

Straight borders Join the borders in the order shown in above diagram.

Begin by measuring the length of the quilt through the centre. Cut two border strips to this length. Mark the halves and quarters of one quilt side and one border with pins. Placing right sides together and matching the pins, stitch quilt and border together, easing the quilt side to fit where necessary. Repeat on the opposite side.

Measure the width of the quilt through the centre, including the borders. Cut two border strips to this measurement and add these borders in the same manner. Add the second border, if any, in the same order as the first.

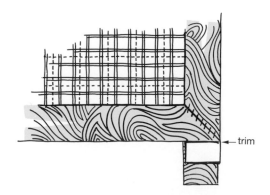

Binding

A double-fold French binding gives a professional finish whether you are using straight or bias binding. If your quilt has curved edges you must use bias binding; either straight or bias binding can be used if your quilt has straight sides.

1 Trim the excess backing and wadding so that the edges are even with the top of the quilt. If the binding is more than 2 in (5 cm) wide, leave the wadding and backing slightly larger than the quilt top.

2 Prepare sufficient binding to go around your quilt plus approximately 6 in (15 cm) for the corners and overlapping the ends. Cut the strips 2 to 4 in (5 to 10 cm) wide. With wrong sides together, press the binding in half lengthwise.

3 On the right side of the quilt and starting about 12 in (30 cm) from one corner, align the edges of the binding with the edge of the quilt and pin, then stitch with a ¼ in (5 mm) seam allowance. At the first corner stop ¼ in (5 mm) from the

edge of the fabric and backstitch. Fold as shown in diagram A, then fold again as shown in diagram B. Continue all around the quilt working each corner in the same way. When you come to the starting point cut the binding, fold under the cut edge and overlap at the starting point. Blindstitch the binding together.

4 Fold over the binding to the back of the quilt to the stitching line. Stitch securely using a blind stitch (diagram C). Stitch the corners as shown in diagram D.

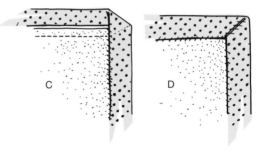

To make continuous bias binding

1 On a square of fabric mark the centre of the width on two opposite sides. Cut the fabric in half diagonally.

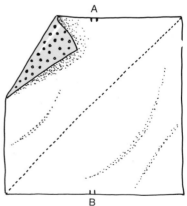

2 With right sides together join the two triangles, matching the points you have marked. Press seam open.

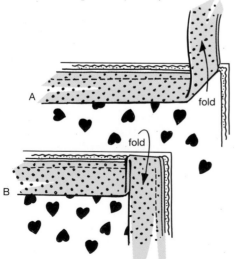

3 On the wrong side of the fabric rule parallel lines across the longest length the desired width of the binding (including seam allowances).

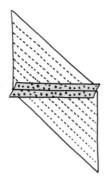

4 With right sides together, stitch the two short sides (marked A and B) together to form a sleeve, dropping down one bias width at the top and the bottom and matching the marked lines with pins. Press seam open.

5 Cut along the marked lines to form one continuous bias strip.

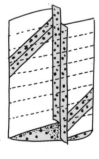
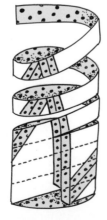

To calculate fabric quantity for making continuous bias binding

To find what size square you need to start with to give you sufficient bias binding for your project:

1 Multiply the length of bias you need by the width you plan to cut the bias.

2 Find the square root.

Example: For a 72 x 72 in quilt you will need 288 in of binding.
a) Multiply 288 x 3 in (binding width) = 864 square inches
b) The square root of 864 is 29.39
Start with a 31 in square to give yourself enough for the overlap and give a margin for error.

Or in metric: for a 185 cm square quilt you will need 740 cm of binding so, 740 x 7.5 cm (binding width) = 5550. The square root of 5550 is 74.5. Start with an 80 cm square.

If you already have a square of fabric and want to know how much bias it will yield, multiply two sides together and divide by the width of the bias you wish to cut.

Example: 36 in square of fabric
a) 36 × 36 = 1296 in
b) 1296 in divided by 3 (bias width) = 432 in
Therefore you will have 432 in (12 yards) of 3 in bias.

Or in metric: 100 cm (or 1 metre) square: 100 x 100 = 10,000 cm ÷ 7.5 (bias width) = 1333 cm (13.3 m) of 7.5 cm bias

NOTES

NOTES

USEFUL TIPS

Tea Dyeing This is an effective way of giving an antique look to cotton fabric. Put 4 tea bags in 1 gallon (4.5 litres) water and bring to boil. Boil for 10 minutes, then remove tea bags. Put in approximately 1 yard (1 metre) wet, pre-washed fabric and simmer in tea for 15 to 30 minutes depending on how dark you wish the fabric to be. Transfer to a setting solution of ½ cup white vinegar to 1 gallon (4.5 litres) water and leave for 10 minutes. Rinse thoroughly. Dry in a tumble dryer or iron dry.

Thread Right-handed people should always thread the needle while the thread is still on the reel, then cut. Left-handed people should cut the thread first and thread the cut end. This prevents knotting and twisting. Never have your thread more than 18 in (45 cm) long.

Thread needles in daylight. Thread a whole packet and leave them attached to the spool, without cutting any lengths of thread. When you wish to use one, pull the thread and the first needle to the desired length, while holding the others back.

Thread has a left twist. Cut the thread at an angle, left to right, and it will be easier to thread.

When quilting, have a long tail of thread and move the needle along as you go, so that the eye of the needle isn't in the same position on the thread all the time. The thread is weakened if the needle is always in the same place.

Magnetic Seam Guide (which should only be used with non-electronic sewing machines) or masking tape placed in front of the presser foot will assure consistent ¼ in (5 mm) seam allowances. Remember in all machine piecing use a *scant* ¼ in (5 mm) seam allowance.

Spy holes (sold as a home security device) can be bought cheaply and can be used instead of reducing glasses for seeing the overall effect of fabrics.

Mirror Tiles Two mirror tiles held at right angles to a block will show it repeated. Often it is difficult to imagine what a quilt will look like from only one block and this is a quick way to see it repeated.

Multi-View Lense When you hold this up to one of your blocks it will be repeated 25 times, so you can see how your finished quilt will look.

Photocopy small pieces of fabric together and this will show up the contrast value between them.

Rotary Cutter If your cutter is no longer running smoothly and the blade is still good, try a few drops of machine oil on it. Keep cutters stored in old spectacles cases for protection.

A **Pinboard** covered with flannelette or curtain interlining is a useful design aid as your blocks and fabric will stick to it without being pinned.

Pressing This is of paramount importance at every stage in patchwork. General rules are: press towards the darker

fabric and press so that adjoining seams go in opposite directions to create less bulk.

When pressing a set of strips, place strips across the ironing board wrong side up with the darker strip on the left. Hold the fabric with the left hand, iron from the right pressing the seams towards the left. Turn the strips over and press on the right side of the fabric in the same manner. This will prevent folds in the seams.

Butting Seams When butting seams together in machine piecing try to have the top scam facing the foot of your machine and the bottom seam facing you.

Machine Stitching Machine needles should be replaced after approximately 4 hours of heavy sewing, such as satin stitch, or after 8 hours normal sewing.

When machine stitching a bias edge to a straight edge, try to stitch with the bias piece on the bottom. If it's on top the machine foot will stretch it by pushing the fabric ahead.

Cleaning Biro stains can sometimes be removed with a hair spray. Spray the area well and blot dry. Repeat until the stain has disappeared, then rinse.

Rust spots can be removed by sponging the area with lemon juice, then holding it over steam from a kettle. (Keep fingers out of the way.) Rinse after treatment.

To remove pets' hairs and threads use sticky tape.

If you prick your finger and stain the quilt, blood stains can be removed straight away with your own saliva.

Fingers Protect your quilting fingers with plasters.

Stencils Make quilting stencils out of self-adhesive shelf paper. Cut a small piece out of the backing paper and stick the stencil to the quilt, then quilt around it. When this is no longer adhesive, another piece of backing can be cut out. This method is ideal if you haven't marked your quilting designs before joining layers together.

Greaseproof Paper makes excellent tracing paper.

Tracing on Net Trace quilting designs on net and lay the net on the quilt. Draw over the design with a marking pencil creating a fine dotted line on the quilt.

Sandpaper or Masking Tape attached to templates and rulers prevents them from slipping on the fabric.

Sticky marks left on fabric by masking or other sticky tape can be removed with white spirit. Rinse afterwards.

Scissors Put a padlock on your fabric scissors to stop the family using them!

Dating It is important that all quilts, however small, are signed and dated either on the front making a feature of it or on the back. Also put some interesting details about the quilt, why it was made, its title, who it was made for and how long it took.

Tacking Use a spoon to help push the needle up when tacking a quilt.

Gathering To gather fabric, lay some narrow piping cord or fine string on the line to be gathered and secure one end. Set sewing machine to an open zig zag and stitch over the cord making sure you don't catch it with your stitches. Pull the cord and your fabric is gathered. Fasten the cord at the other end.

Fabric Shopping If you find yourself in a quilt shop and are tempted to buy some fabric without any particular design in mind, buy ½ yard (0.5 metre) of fabrics that just look good, 1 yard (1 metre) of ones you can't live without, 2 yards (2 metres) of ones that are a good background, 2½ yards (2.5 metres) of border fabrics and 5 yards (5 metres) of backing fabrics. Bear in mind that between 9 and 10 yards (metres) in total are needed for a double quilt, 6 yards (metres) for a single and 2-3 yards (metres) for a cot. Remember that fabric purchases cannot always be repeated and think of the wonderful scrap quilts you can make with any leftovers.

NOTES

NOTES

DATE STARTED: .... DATE FINISHED: ....

BLOCK DESIGN: QUILTING DESIGN:

QUILT SIZE: .... BLOCK SIZE: ....

NO. OF BLOCKS REQUIRED: ....

BORDERS: ....

SASHING: ....

TEMPLATES USED:

SHAPE	SIZE	NUMBER PER BLOCK	NUMBER PER QUILT

FABRICS USED & AMOUNT REQUIRED:

	A	B	C	D	E

WADDING USED: ....

DESTINATION OF QUILT WHEN COMPLETE: ....

NOTES: ....

....

DATE STARTED: .... DATE FINISHED: ....

BLOCK DESIGN: QUILTING DESIGN:

QUILT SIZE: ....   BLOCK SIZE: ....

NO. OF BLOCKS REQUIRED: ....

BORDERS: ....

SASHING: ....

TEMPLATES USED:

SHAPE	SIZE	NUMBER PER BLOCK	NUMBER PER QUILT

FABRICS USED & AMOUNT REQUIRED:

	A	B	C	D	E

WADDING USED: ....

DESTINATION OF QUILT WHEN COMPLETE: ....

NOTES: ....
....
....

DATE STARTED: .... DATE FINISHED: ....

BLOCK DESIGN: QUILTING DESIGN:

QUILT SIZE: .... BLOCK SIZE: ....

NO. OF BLOCKS REQUIRED: ....

BORDERS: ....

SASHING: ....

TEMPLATES USED:

SHAPE	SIZE	NUMBER PER BLOCK	NUMBER PER QUILT

FABRICS USED & AMOUNT REQUIRED:

A	B	C	D	E

WADDING USED: ....

DESTINATION OF QUILT WHEN COMPLETE: ....

NOTES: ....

....

DATE STARTED: .... DATE FINISHED: ....

BLOCK DESIGN: QUILTING DESIGN:

QUILT SIZE: .... BLOCK SIZE: ....

NO. OF BLOCKS REQUIRED: ....

BORDERS: ....

SASHING: ....

TEMPLATES USED:

SHAPE	SIZE	NUMBER PER BLOCK	NUMBER PER QUILT

FABRICS USED & AMOUNT REQUIRED:

A	B	C	D	E

WADDING USED: ....

DESTINATION OF QUILT WHEN COMPLETE: ....

NOTES: ....

....

DATE STARTED: ....

DATE FINISHED: ....

BLOCK DESIGN:

QUILTING DESIGN:

QUILT SIZE: ....

BLOCK SIZE: ....

NO. OF BLOCKS REQUIRED: ....

BORDERS: ....

SASHING: ....

TEMPLATES USED:

SHAPE	SIZE	NUMBER PER BLOCK	NUMBER PER QUILT

FABRICS USED & AMOUNT REQUIRED:

A	B	C	D	E

WADDING USED: ....

DESTINATION OF QUILT WHEN COMPLETE: ....

NOTES:

DATE STARTED: .... DATE FINISHED: ....

BLOCK DESIGN: QUILTING DESIGN:

QUILT SIZE: .... BLOCK SIZE: ....

NO. OF BLOCKS REQUIRED: ....

BORDERS: ....

SASHING: ....

TEMPLATES USED:

SHAPE	SIZE	NUMBER PER BLOCK	NUMBER PER QUILT

FABRICS USED & AMOUNT REQUIRED:

A	B	C	D	E

WADDING USED: ....

DESTINATION OF QUILT WHEN COMPLETE: ....

NOTES: ....

....

DATE STARTED: .... DATE FINISHED: ....

BLOCK DESIGN: QUILTING DESIGN:

QUILT SIZE: .... BLOCK SIZE: ....

NO. OF BLOCKS REQUIRED: ....

BORDERS: ....

SASHING: ....

TEMPLATES USED:

SHAPE	SIZE	NUMBER PER BLOCK	NUMBER PER QUILT

FABRICS USED & AMOUNT REQUIRED:

A	B	C	D	E

WADDING USED: ....

DESTINATION OF QUILT WHEN COMPLETE: ....

NOTES: ....
....

DATE STARTED: .... DATE FINISHED: ....

BLOCK DESIGN: QUILTING DESIGN:

QUILT SIZE: .... BLOCK SIZE: ....

NO. OF BLOCKS REQUIRED: ....

BORDERS: ....

SASHING: ....

TEMPLATES USED:

SHAPE	SIZE	NUMBER PER BLOCK	NUMBER PER QUILT

FABRICS USED & AMOUNT REQUIRED:

A	B	C	D	E

WADDING USED: ....

DESTINATION OF QUILT WHEN COMPLETE: ....

NOTES: ....

....

DATE STARTED: .... DATE FINISHED: ....

BLOCK DESIGN: QUILTING DESIGN:

QUILT SIZE: .... BLOCK SIZE: ....

NO. OF BLOCKS REQUIRED: ....

BORDERS: ....

SASHING: ....

TEMPLATES USED:

SHAPE	SIZE	NUMBER PER BLOCK	NUMBER PER QUILT

FABRICS USED & AMOUNT REQUIRED:

A	B	C	D	E

WADDING USED: ....

DESTINATION OF QUILT WHEN COMPLETE: ....

NOTES: ....
....

DATE STARTED: .... DATE FINISHED: ....

BLOCK DESIGN: QUILTING DESIGN:

QUILT SIZE: .... BLOCK SIZE: ....

NO. OF BLOCKS REQUIRED: ....

BORDERS: ....

SASHING: ....

TEMPLATES USED:

SHAPE	SIZE	NUMBER PER BLOCK	NUMBER PER QUILT

FABRICS USED & AMOUNT REQUIRED:

A	B	C	D	E

WADDING USED: ....

DESTINATION OF QUILT WHEN COMPLETE: ....

NOTES: ....
....
....

CONVERTING YARDS TO METRES

The following table gives metric conversions which have been rounded up
to the nearest 0.10 metre.

Yards	Metres	Yards	Metres	Yards	Metres	Yards	Metres	Yards	Metres
$^1/_8$	0.20	$2^1/_8$	2.00	$4^1/_8$	3.80	$6^1/_8$	5.60	$8^1/_8$	7.50
$^1/_4$	0.30	$2^1/_4$	2.10	$4^1/_4$	3.90	$6^1/_4$	5.80	$8^1/_4$	7.60
$^3/_8$	0.40	$2^3/_8$	2.20	$4^3/_8$	4.00	$6^3/_8$	5.90	$7^3/_8$	7.70
$^1/_2$	0.50	$2^1/_2$	2.30	$4^1/_2$	4.20	$6^1/_2$	6.00	$8^1/_2$	7.80
$^5/_8$	0.60	$2^5/_8$	2.40	$4^5/_8$	4.30	$6^5/_8$	6.10	$8^5/_8$	7.90
$^3/_4$	0.70	$2^3/_4$	2.60	$4^3/_4$	4.40	$6^3/_4$	6.20	$8^3/_4$	8.00
$^7/_8$	0.80	$2^7/_8$	2.70	$4^7/_8$	4.50	$6^7/_8$	6.30	$8^7/_8$	8.20
1	1.00	3	2.80	5	4.60	7	6.40	9	8.30
$1^1/_8$	1.10	$3^1/_8$	2.90	$5^1/_8$	4.70	$7^1/_8$	6.60	$9^1/_8$	8.40
$1^1/_4$	1.20	$3^1/_4$	3.00	$5^1/_4$	4.80	$7^1/_4$	6.70	$9^1/_4$	8.50
$1^3/_8$	1.30	$3^3/_8$	3.10	$5^3/_8$	5.00	$7^3/_8$	6.80	$9^3/_8$	8.60
$1^1/_2$	1.40	$3^1/_2$	3.20	$5^1/_2$	5.10	$7^1/_2$	6.90	$9^1/_2$	8.70
$1^5/_8$	1.50	$3^5/_8$	3.40	$5^5/_8$	5.20	$7^5/_8$	7.00	$9^5/_8$	8.80
$1^3/_4$	1.60	$3^3/_4$	3.50	$5^3/_4$	5.30	$7^3/_4$	7.10	$9^3/_4$	9.00
$1^7/_8$	1.80	$3^7/_8$	3.60	$5^7/_8$	5.40	$7^7/_8$	7.20	$9^7/_8$	9.10
2	1.90	4	3.70	6	5.50	8	7.40	10	9.20

Metric Conversion
1 metre = 39.37 inches
1 inch = 2.54 centimetres
yards × 0.9144 = metres
inches × 2.54 = centimetres
metres ÷ 0.9144 = yards
centimetres ÷ 2.54 = inches

Fractions of a yard converted to decimals
$^1/_8$ yard = 0.125 yard
$^1/_4$ yard = 0.25 yard
$^3/_8$ yard = 0.375 yard
$^1/_2$ yard = 0.5 yard
$^5/_8$ yard = 0.625 yard
$^3/_4$ yard = 0.75 yard
$^7/_8$ yard = 0.875 yard